SAYINGS and PHRASES

Break a Leg!

(And Other Odd Things We Say)

written by Cynthia Klingel ★ illustrated by Mernie Gallagher-Cole

ABOUT THE AUTHOR

As a high school English teacher and as an elementary teacher, Cynthia Klingel has shared her love of language with students. She has always been fascinated with idioms and figures of speech. Today Cynthia is a school district administrator in Minnesota. She has two daughters who also share her love of language through reading, writing, and talking!

ABOUT THE ILLUSTRATOR

Mernie Gallagher-Cole lives in Pennsylvania with her husband and two children. She uses sayings and phrases like the ones in this book every day. She has illustrated many children's books, including *Messy Molly* and *Día De Los Muertos* for The Child's World®.

The Child's World®

Published in the United States of America by The Child's World®
1980 Lookout Drive • Mankato, MN 56003-1705
800-599-READ • www.childsworld.com

ACKNOWLEDGMENTS
The Child's World®: Mary Berendes, Publishing Director

Katherine Stevenson: Editing

The Design Lab: Kathleen Petelinsek, Design; Victoria Stanley, Page Production

LIBRARY OF CONGRESS CATALOGING-IN-PUBLICATION DATA
Klingel, Cynthia Fitterer.
  Break a leg! (and other odd things we say) / by Cynthia Klingel.
    p. cm. — (Sayings and phrases)
  ISBN 978-1-60253-205-2 (library bound : alk. paper)
  1. English language—Idioms—Juvenile literature.
2. Figures of speech—Juvenile literature. I. Title.
II. Series.
PE1460.K6833 2009
428.1—dc22   2009001638

People use idioms
(ID-ee-umz) every day.
These are sayings and
phrases with meanings that
are different from the actual
words. Some idioms seem silly.
Many of them don't make
much sense . . . at first.

This book will help you
understand some of the most
common idioms. It will tell
you how you might hear a
saying or phrase. It will tell
you what the saying really
means. All of these sayings
and short phrases—even the
silly ones—are an important
part of our language!

TABLE of CONTENTS

Break a leg

Cora had the lead in the school play. She knew all her lines, but she was still nervous. The first performance was about to start. She took a deep breath to calm herself. The director walked by to check Cora's costume for the last time. Then he gave Cora a big grin and said, "You're all set. Break a leg!"

MEANING: A way of wishing a performer well. It comes from the idea that saying "Good luck!" to actors brings them bad luck—so you wish them bad luck instead!

Chew the fat

It was lunchtime, and Stuart was hungry. His mom had stepped outside a little while ago. Finally she came back in.

"Hi, Mom," said Stuart. "Could we make lunch? I'm starved!"

"Sure!" said his mom with a smile. "Sorry I took so long. I was chewing the fat with the neighbors. They just got back from vacation, and I wanted to hear how it went."

MEANING: To talk or chat with someone

Come to a head

Jonathan's brother Rob wasn't in a good mood. He'd just come from baseball practice.

"What's the matter?" Jonathan asked.

"Oh," said Rob, "Zach and Michael got really mad and yelled at each other. They haven't been getting along very well lately. Today everything came to a head."

MEANING: When a situation has been developing and finally reaches a crisis point

Down to the wire

Chris and Rachel were helping their friend Samantha run for class president. She was running against a boy named Matthew. Both of the candidates were very popular.

"What a close race!" said Chris, as he put up a "Vote for Samantha!" poster. "Do you think Samantha is going to win?"

"I don't know," said Rachel. "I think it's going to go right down to the wire."

MEANING: A close race, where the winner is decided at the last minute. The "wire" refers to the finish line in horse racing.

Easy as pie

Jordan and Sue went canoeing for the first time with their Uncle Mark. He showed them how to paddle and steer, and they paddled happily all over the lake.

"How was it?" asked Aunt Tess as the three came in for lunch.

"Great!" said Sue. "It's so much fun!"

"It isn't hard, either," said Jordan. "In fact, it's as easy as pie!"

MEANING: Very easy to do

Fly-by-night

Tim's neighbor, Mr. Russell, had just hired a company to put a new front door on his house. When Tim came outside, Mr. Russell was looking at the door with a frown on his face.

"What's wrong?" Tim asked.

"They didn't do a very good job," said Mr. Russell. "And now I can't get them to fix it. What a fly-by-night company!"

MEANING: Someone who doesn't do things well and might not stay in business for long

Get into the swing of things

Josh had been sick, and it was his first day back at school. He had so much catching up to do! He couldn't believe how much he had missed.

"Don't be discouraged," said his dad at dinner that night. "You've been gone a week. It'll take you a few days to get back in the swing of things."

MEANING: To feel comfortable doing something

Graveyard shift

Rachel ran into the house. "I'm home," she hollered as she slammed the door.

Her dad looked up from reading his book. "Shhhh, Rachel. Your mom's still sleeping."

"Why is she sleeping?" asked Rachel. "It's almost lunchtime!"

"One of the people she works with got sick last night," explained Dad. "So your mom went in and worked the graveyard shift."

MEANING: A block of time that somebody works at night

Heart of gold

Katie had a great birthday. She and her family went to the lake, and then out for pizza. When they got home, Katie's mom handed her a card.

"Oh!" exclaimed Katie, as she opened the card. "It's got penguins on it! Aunt Laurie always remembers what I like."

"Laurie has a heart of gold," Katie's mom agreed.

MEANING: Used to describe someone who is kind, thinks of others, and does nice things for people

Hit the hay

Erica was curled up on the sofa. She wanted to see the end of the movie, but she was getting really sleepy.

"You look like you're ready for bed," said her mom.

"I think I can make it to the end," said Erica.

"No, let's watch the rest tomorrow," said Dad. "Right now, it's time for you to hit the hay."

MEANING: To go to bed

In a nutshell

Kyle's family was hoping to move from their small apartment into a house. They'd found one they really liked, with a park nearby and a great yard. Kyle's parents were meeting with the owner. When they came home, Kyle and his sisters were waiting.

"How did it go? Did we get it?" they asked excitedly.

"In a nutshell," said Dad, "we're moving!"

MEANING: To give a short answer or just the basic information

Keep a straight face

Hic
Hic
Hic

Rebecca's class had a really nice song to sing in the spring concert. Just as they started, Rebecca heard a "Hic!" right behind her. Oh no, Erik had the hiccups! Somehow Rebecca kept herself from laughing while they finished the song.

"So that's what happened," her friend Annie said later. "I knew something was going on. I don't know how you kept a straight face!"

MEANING: To keep yourself from laughing

Knock on wood

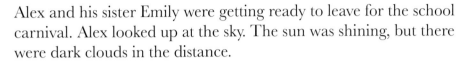

Alex and his sister Emily were getting ready to leave for the school carnival. Alex looked up at the sky. The sun was shining, but there were dark clouds in the distance.

"I hope it doesn't rain," Alex said.

"It won't," said Emily. "It's going to be a really nice day—knock on wood!"

MEANING: This saying is supposed to keep something that you're talking about from going wrong. Some people knock on furniture or other wood as they say this.

Like a bump on a log

It was a hot summer day, and Toby was feeling lazy. His sister asked him to go on a bike ride. His brother wanted him to go skateboarding. But Toby just wanted to sit on the couch, watching TV.

"All right, Toby," said Dad as he walked into the room. "Time to get moving. You've been sitting there all afternoon, like a bump on a log."

MEANING: Sitting and doing nothing

On pins and needles

Sarah loved playing basketball. She practiced shooting baskets all the time. This morning she had tried out for the team. Now she was waiting to hear whether she made it.

"I hope I hear soon!" Sarah said to her friend Brittany. "I'm really nervous. I can't even think about anything else."

"I'll bet!" said Brittany. "You must be on pins and needles."

MEANING: Feeling nervous. It comes from the uncomfortable tingling feeling people sometimes get.

Out of the frying pan and into the fire

Jason was writing an adventure story. The hero had just escaped from evil aliens, and Jason wasn't sure what should come next.

"Well," said his dad, "how about putting him in even greater danger?"

"Hmmm," said Jason, thinking hard. "So he escapes from the aliens and thinks he's safe, but then—look out! Things get even worse!"

"Yup," said Dad. "Out of the frying pan and into the fire."

MEANING: To get out of a bad situation only to end up in an even worse one

Pass the buck

Everybody was getting ready for the school party. Ms. Flynn's class was putting up decorations.

"Hey, Joey," said Nathaniel, from his perch on a stepstool. "Could you please get the streamers?"

"Nope, that's not my job," answered Joey. "Ask Emma."

"It's not my job, either," Emma said. "Try Kaitlin."

"Come on, you guys," Nathaniel said with a sigh. "Please, somebody grab the streamers, and quit passing the buck!"

MEANING: To hand a responsibility on to someone else; to have someone else make a decision

Play it by ear

Tomorrow was the Fourth of July, and Angela's family was trying to decide what to do.

"We could go to the fireworks," suggested Hannah.

"We could go to the lake," said Maria.

"There's a big parade in town," suggested Mom. "That's always fun."

"The weather forecast says it might rain," said Dad. "Let's see what it's like tomorrow morning and then play it by ear."

MEANING: To wait and see what happens; to make plans as you go

Pull your leg

Amy and her little brother Brandon were spending time with their grandpa. Brandon was showing Grandpa what a terrible face he could make.

"Careful, Brandon," said Grandpa. "If you so that too often, your face will stay that way!"

"Really?" said Brandon, his eyes wide.

"Oh Grandpa, you used to tell me that, too," Amy said with a laugh. "Don't worry, Brandon, Grandpa's just pulling your leg."

MEANING: To tease people by telling them something that isn't true

The real McCoy

Ben just gotten home from a baseball game at the stadium. He was very excited!

"Hey Carl," he said to his brother. "Take a look at this!" He held up a baseball.

"Did you catch a ball?" cried Carl.

"I sure did. I got it signed, too!" Ben exclaimed.

"Wow!" said Carl. "It that really Orlando Jackson's autograph?"

"Yup," said Ben. "It's the real McCoy."

MEANING: The real thing, not a fake or a copy

Sick as a dog

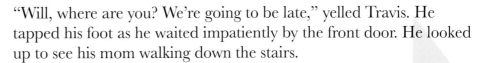

"Will, where are you? We're going to be late," yelled Travis. He tapped his foot as he waited impatiently by the front door. He looked up to see his mom walking down the stairs.

"Where's Will? We're going to be late for school if we don't leave now!" said Travis.

"Will is staying home today. He's sick as a dog!" answered Mom.

MEANING: Very sick

19

Spitting image

Joy's grandma lived far away, and Joy didn't get to see her very often. Finally, Grandma was coming for a visit. Joy was excited! She rode along to the airport to pick her up. When the passengers got off the plane, Joy was waiting. She ran to her grandma the second she saw her.

"Why, Joy!" said Grandma with a laugh. "You're the spitting image of your Aunt Kristin!"

MEANING: Someone who looks very much like someone else

Sweet tooth

Sam and his sister were at a picnic. There was a table full of tasty food—hamburgers, hot dogs, chips, potato salad, and lots more. They finished off one plateful and went back for more.

"Look what Maddy's up to," said Sam. "All she's been eating are brownies, cookies, and cake."

"I know," said Sam's sister. "That kid really has a sweet tooth!"

MEANING: A liking for sweet foods

Throw in the towel

Jenna's soccer team had lost their last three games. The other teams had outscored them easily. Jenna wasn't looking forward to playing today. "Maybe we should just quit," she said to her teammate.

The girls gathered around their coach before the game. "All right," the coach said. "I know you've lost some games, and I'm sure you feel like throwing in the towel. But I believe you can win this one!"

MEANING: To quit or give up

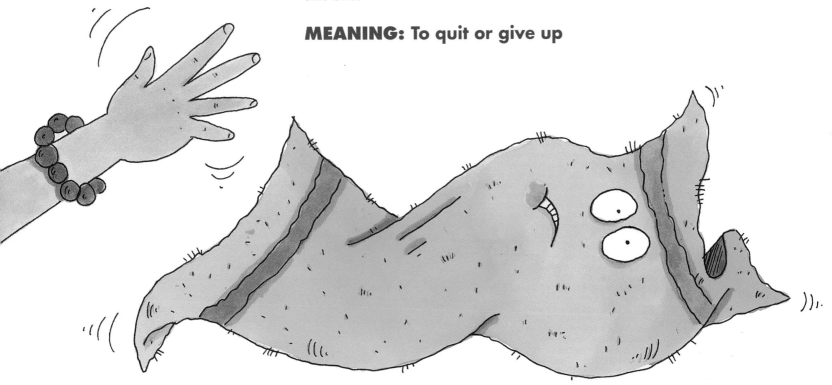

Two cents' worth

Dana, Kristal, and Gina couldn't decide what to do.

"My mom said she'd take us to a movie," said Dana.

"It's nice today," said Kristal. "I'd rather go to the park and play."

"We do that all the time," said Dana.

"Excuse me," said Gina. "Could I put in my two cents' worth? I think we should do both."

MEANING: Your opinion; what you think about something

When in Rome

"This is weird," whispered Tim. "Where's the butter? Where's the syrup?" He stared at his waffle. He and his family were on vacation, eating breakfast in a restaurant far from home.

"See the toppings in those dishes?" asked his dad. "You put those on your waffle."

"That's weird," Tim said again. "Why don't they make them like we do at home?"

"Come on, give it a try," said Dad. "When in Rome...."

MEANING: The full saying is, "When in Rome, do as the Romans do." This means that when you're in another place, you should try things the way people do them there.

You can lead a horse to water

Jessica was growing flowers in the backyard, and some were falling over. She was putting in a stick to hold them up, pounding it into the ground with a rock she found nearby.

"Would you like to borrow a hammer?" asked Mrs. McGill, who lived next door.

"No thanks," said Jessica. "I'll just keep doing this."

"Well," said Mrs. McGill with a smile, "you can lead a horse to water...."

MEANING: The full saying is, "You can lead a horse to water, but you can't make it drink." It means that you can show people something that would help them, but you can't make them take it.

WATER